This book
belongs to...

_____

To Ste x

OXFORD
UNIVERSITY PRESS

Great Clarendon Street, Oxford OX2 6DP

Oxford University Press is a department of the University of Oxford.
It furthers the University's objective of excellence in research, scholarship,
and education by publishing worldwide in

Oxford New York

Auckland Bangkok Buenos Aires Cape Town Chennai
Dar es Salaam Delhi Hong Kong Istanbul Karachi Kolkata
Kuala Lumpur Madrid Melbourne Mexico City Mumbai Nairobi
São Paulo Shanghai Taipei Tokyo Toronto

Oxford is a registered trade mark of Oxford University Press
in the UK and in certain other countries

British Library Cataloguing in Publication Data available

ISBN 0 19 279131 1 Hardback
ISBN 0 19 272568 8 Paperback

10 9 8 7 6 5 4 3 2 1

Printed in China

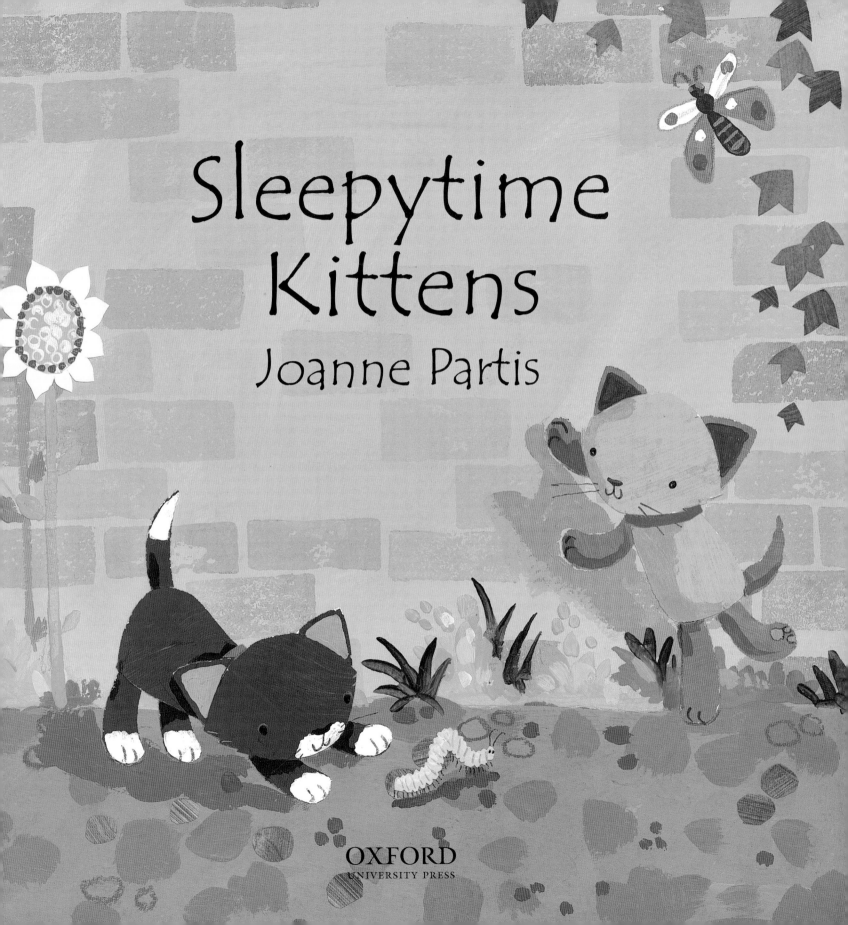

Sleepytime
Kittens

Joanne Partis

OXFORD
UNIVERSITY PRESS

It was a warm summer's evening down on the farm.

In the farmhouse ...

... three little kittens didn't feel sleepy. 'When you can't sleep, you need to count sheep,' said Mum.

So the three little kittens set out
to find some sheep to count.

They found...

One shaggy sheepdog.
Woof!

But no sheep.

Two munching cows.

Crunch!

Munch! But no sheep.

Three playful foxes.

Four bouncy rabbits.

Boing!
Boing! Boing!

Boing!
Boing!

But no sheep.

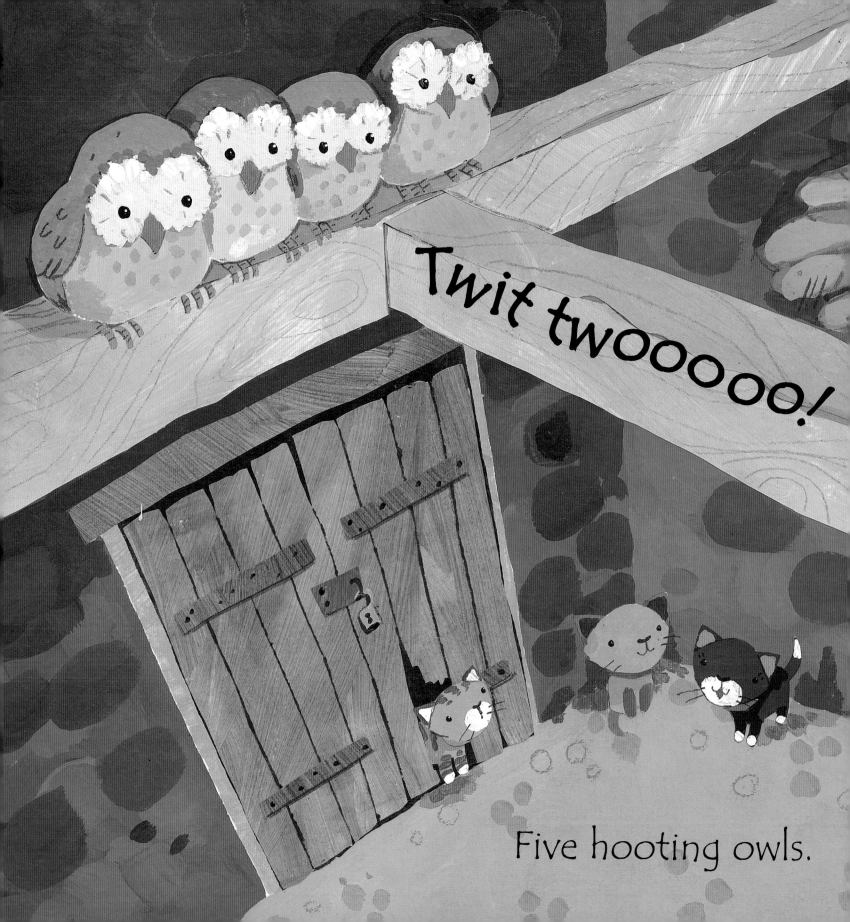

Twit twooooo!

Five hooting owls.

Twit twooooo!

But no sheep.

Six friendly pigs.

Oink! Oink! Oink!

Oink! Oink! Oink!

But no sheep.

Seven chirping chickens.

Cluck! Cluck!

Cluck!

Cluck!

Cluck!

But no sheep.

Quack!

Quack!

Eight noisy ducks.

Quack! Quack!

But no sheep.

Quack!

Nine nervous mice.

Squeak! Squeak! Squeak!

Squeak! Squeak!

But no sheep.

Squeak!

Squeak!

By now the kittens had counted
so many things that at last
they felt sleepy.

They stretched,

and yawned,

and snuggled down in the soft grass.
But they weren't the only ones in the field ...

I'm on every page. Can you find me?

Baa!